The Shepherd's Son

Robert Van de Weyer

Illustrated by Annabel Spenceley

At dawn, on the very first Christmas morning, a shepherd living near Bethlehem burst into his cottage.

"Wake up! Wake up!" he cried to his wife and son, who were still tucked warmly in bed. "A most amazing thing happened last night! I was looking after our sheep, when suddenly a bright light shone across the sky. Then a voice started speaking."

"What did it say?" asked his son, who was now sitting upright in bed, his mouth wide open.

"It told us to go into Bethlehem to see a little
baby that had just been born – a baby who would
save the world." He went on to describe how he
and the other shepherds had rushed to Bethlehem
and seen the baby Jesus lying in a manger, with his
parents, Mary and Joseph, beside him.

"I'd like to take a present to the baby Jesus,"
said the shepherd's son, who was called Benjamin.

"That would be very nice," said his mother,
"but we've no money for you to buy a present.
You'll have to go out and find something."

As Benjamin got up and had his breakfast, he wondered what he could find to give to Jesus. After breakfast he walked out into the fields, where the cold wind whipped around his body. He continued wracking his brain to think of something. Suddenly he spotted white, fluffy pieces of sheep's wool caught on a hedge — and he realized what he must give to Jesus.

Throughout that day – the first Christmas
Day – Benjamin walked around the fields near his
home, gathering all the pieces of wool that the
sheep had left behind when their fleece had caught
on the thorns and thistles. After supper he sewed a
bag out of a piece of cloth. Then he stuffed the
wool into the bag to make a big, soft pillow for
Jesus to rest his head on.

That night as he lay in bed, his heart thumped with excitement as he looked forward to going to Bethlehem and giving his pillow to Jesus. At last he fell asleep. He woke up at the crack of dawn, leaped out of bed, and quickly swallowed his breakfast. Then he put the pillow under his arm and set off for Bethlehem. It was a long journey for his little legs, so he knew he must hurry if he was to get there and back before nightfall.

After about a mile he met a small girl sitting on a log beside the road. In her hands she was clutching a tiny bird that was shivering with cold.

"What's wrong with that baby bird?" asked Benjamin.

"The poor thing has lost its mother," the girl replied, "and it's dying of cold."

Benjamin looked at his pillow full of wool. Then he looked at the tiny bird. The bird was cheeping as if it were begging Benjamin for help. Each cheep was softer than the last, as its frail body grew weaker. Benjamin had wanted to give all the wool to Jesus, yet he could not let the baby bird die. So he opened the pillow and took out enough wool to wrap around the bird. Gradually, as the bird grew warmer, its cheep became stronger and happier.

Benjamin continued on his way. A mile farther on he met an old man with a camel, and on the camel's back was a heavy pack. One corner of the pack was rubbing against the camel's side, causing a nasty sore. The camel was in such pain that it could hardly walk.

Benjamin looked at his pillow of wool. Then he looked at the poor camel. The camel was panting and snorting as if asking for Benjamin's help. Benjamin knew that if he put some of his wool under the pack, he could ease the sore. His heart was torn in two. He so wanted to give Jesus a big, soft pillow, yet he could not bear to see the camel in pain.

His own hands made the decision for him. He found himself reaching into the pillow and taking out a wad of wool. He carefully placed it under the pack where it had been rubbing the camel's skin. At once the camel stopped panting and snorting and started to walk so briskly that the old man could hardly keep up.

"Thank you, little friend," the old man called back. "May God bless you for your kindness."

Benjamin had spent so long with the little bird and the camel that, by the time he could see Bethlehem on the horizon, the sun was already setting. He felt frightened because he knew he would have to sleep in Bethlehem overnight and he had no friends there to stay with. He quickened his pace, hoping to reach the town before nightfall.

A few moments later he saw ahead of him a man leading a donkey, and on the donkey was a young woman with a large cloak drawn around her. They were coming towards him, and as they approached, Benjamin could hear them speaking.

"You must be very uncomfortable sitting on the bare back of the donkey," the man was saying. "If only I had a cushion for you to sit on."

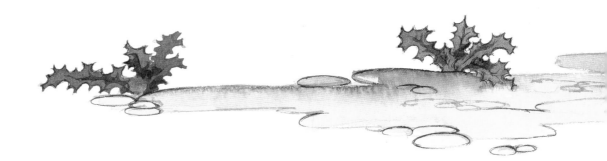

"Don't worry. God will look after us," the woman replied. But her voice sounded so weary that Benjamin forgot his own plight and wanted to try to help her. He knew that he could make her comfortable if he gave her the pillow.

Tears welled up in Benjamin's eyes. "If I give her my pillow, she will be comfortable," he thought. "But then I will have nothing to give to baby Jesus — and my journey will be wasted."

In his heart he knew what he must do. He wiped the tears from his eyes, walked up to the man and woman, and offered his pillow.

"That is most generous!" exclaimed the man.

The woman smiled at Benjamin and climbed
down from the donkey. As she did, Benjamin
caught sight of a tiny baby in her arms under the
cloak. The man put the pillow on the donkey's
back as a saddle.

"Please," said the woman, "could you take a piece of wool from the pillow to put on my shoulder – for baby Jesus to rest his head on?"

Benjamin could hardly believe his ears. He was so amazed that his jaw dropped. He stood speechless, staring at the woman and the tiny baby under her cloak.

"We shall always be grateful to you," said the man. "Thank you, child."

Benjamin stood in the middle of the road, his mouth still wide open, and watched the man, the woman, the donkey, and Jesus disappear over a hill. Then, when they were out of sight, he let out a great yelp of delight and danced all the way to Bethlehem!

All the inns were full by the time he arrived. But a kindly innkeeper allowed him to sleep in his stable with the animals.

"Do you know," said the innkeeper, "that last night a baby was born in this stable? He slept in that manger over there."

So Benjamin went over to the manger and climbed in. There was just enough room to curl up snugly. And even though a cold wind was blowing, the hay in the manger still felt warm, as if Jesus had just been there.

Copyright © 1993 Hunt & Thorpe
Text © 1993 by Robert Van de Weyer
Illustrations © 1993 by Annabel Spenceley
Originally published by Hunt & Thorpe 1993

ISBN 1 85608 150 8

In Australia this book is published by:
Hunt & Thorpe Australia Pty Ltd.
9 Euston Street, Rydalmere NSW 2116

A CIP catalogue record for this book is available from
the British Library

Manufactured in Italy